SCIENCE
MAGIC
WITH SHAPES
& MATERIALS
CHRIS OXLADE

BARRON'S

First edition for the United States, Canada, and the Philippines published 1995 by Barron's Educational Series, Inc.

Design
David West Children's Book Design
Designer
Edward Simkins
Editor
Jim Pipe
Illustrator
Peter Harper
Model Maker
David Millea
Photographer
Roger Vlitos

© Aladdin Books Ltd. 1994
Created and designed by
N.W. Books
28 Percy Street
London W1P 9FF

First published in
Great Britain in 1994 by
Franklin Watts Ltd.
96 Leonard Street
London EC2A 4RH

All inquiries should be addressed to:
Barron's Educational Series, Inc.
250 Wireless Boulevard
Hauppauge, NY 11788

International Standard Book No.
0-8120-6518-2 (hardcover)
0-8120-9369-0 (paperback)

Library of Congress Catalog
Card No. 94-40701

Library of Congress Cataloging-in-Publication Data

Oxlade, Chris.
Science magic with shapes and materials / Chris Oxlade. — 1st ed. for the U.S., Canada, and the Philippines.
p. cm. — (Science magic)
Originally published: London: F. Watts, 1994.
Includes index.
ISBN 0-8120-6518-2. — ISBN 0-8120-9369-0 (pbk.)
1. Conjuring—Juvenile literature.
2. Form perception—Juvenile literature.
3. Scientific recreations—Juvenile literature.
[1. Magic tricks. 2. Form perception.
3. Scientific recreations.] I. Title. II. Series.
GV 1548.0967 1995   94-40701
793.8—dc20   CIP
                          AC

Printed in Belgium
5678 4208 987654321

CONTENTS

MATERIALS MAGIC!

Everyday materials can be a magician's best friend, allowing you to perform fantastic feats and incredible illusions. Each kind of material works better in some situations than in others because of the way in which its molecules are linked to each other. A piece of string, for example, is strong when you pull it, but collapses easily when you push it. Once you know how to use materials, objects will magically disappear into thin air and fragile structures will become extraordinarily strong. So get shapes into your act, and get your act into shape!

BE AN EXPERT MAGICIAN

PREPARING YOUR ROUTINE

There is much more to being a magician than just doing tricks. It is important that you and your assistant practice your whole routine lots of times, so that your performance goes smoothly when you do it for an audience. You will be a more entertaining magician if you do.

PROPS

Props are all the bits and pieces of equipment that a magician uses during an act, including his or her clothes as well as the things needed for the tricks themselves. It's a good idea to make a magician's trunk from a large box to keep all your props in. During your routine, you can dip into the trunk, pulling out all sorts of equipment and crazy objects (see Misdirection). You could also tell jokes about these objects.

PROPS LIST

*Magic wand ★ Top hat
Vest ★ Books ★ Cardboard
Cardboard boxes, tube
Cardboard box with lid
Cellophane tape ★ Ceramic mug
Cloth ★ Clothespins ★ Colored markers
or pens ★ Colored paper ★ Eggs ★ Fishing
line or wire ★ Glass jars with lids ★ Glue ★ Kettle
Large cloth ★ Marbles ★ Modeling clay ★ Newspaper
Paper ★ Paintbrush ★ Paints ★ Pegs ★ Pencil ★ Plastic
bags (small) ★ Plastic bottles, sandwich box, tray ★ Scissors
Small saw ★ Straws ★ Plastic spoons ★ Tissue paper ★ Tray
 Water ★ Wooden dowels or corks ★ Hot water*

WHICH TRICKS?

Work out which tricks you want to include in your routine. Put in some long tricks and some short tricks to keep your audience interested. If you can, include a trick that you can

keep going back to during the routine. Magicians call this a "running gag."

MAGICIAN'S PATTER

Patter is what you say during your routine. Good patter makes a routine much more interesting and allows it to run more smoothly. It is a good way

to entertain your audience during the slower parts of your routine. Try to make up a story for each trick. Remember to introduce yourself and your assistant at the start and to thank your audience at the end. Practice your patter when you practice your tricks.

MISDIRECTION

Misdirection is an important part of a magician's routine. By waving a colorful scarf in the air or telling a joke, you can distract the audience's attention from something you'd rather they didn't see!

KEEP IT SECRET

The best magicians never give away their secrets. If anyone asks how your tricks work, just reply, "By magic!" Then you can impress people with your tricks again and again.

INTRODUCING MAGIC MIKE
AND THE
PAPER BRIDGE

Magic Mike uses his extraordinary powers to transform flimsy paper into a bridge that holds a heavy train.

Start with a flat cardboard bridge supported by the two boxes. When you move the heavy train across the bridge, the bridge collapses under it. Announce that you can change the strength of the cardboard. Just fold it into ridges, and Abracadabra! — it supports the train.

WHAT YOU NEED
Small cardboard boxes
Thin cardboard
Colored paper
Scissors ★ Paints
Paintbrush
Cellophane tape
Marbles

THE SCIENCE BEHIND THE TRICK

The cardboard makes a simple beam bridge between the supports. The weight of the train tries to bend it. The amount the beam bends depends on its shape. When you fold the cardboard into ridges you form triangular shapes, which are much stronger than the flat cardboard.

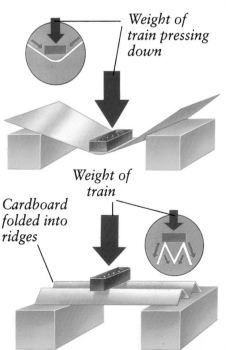

Weight of train pressing down

Weight of train

Cardboard folded into ridges

1 Decorate two cardboard boxes and a piece of cardboard — about 20 in. (50 cm) by 12 in. (30 cm) — with magic symbols cut from colored paper.

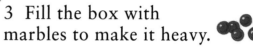

2 Paint wheels and windows on a small cardboard box so that it looks like a train.

3 Fill the box with marbles to make it heavy.

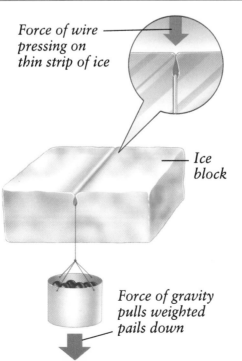

INTRODUCING MAGIC MANDY
AND THE
SLICE THROUGH ICE

It's incredible! Magic Mandy cuts through the ice block, but it's still in one piece.

Ask your assistant to bring in the ice block. (Leave it in the freezer until the last moment.) Lay it between the jar supports. Put the wire over the block with one pail on each side. Fill the pails with marbles to weigh the wire down. The trick takes a while to work, so do another trick while you wait. The wire will gradually move through the block, yet the ice will remain in one piece!

WHAT YOU NEED
Plastic sandwich box
Colored paper ★ Glue
Scissors ★ Glass jars with
lids ★ Plastic bottles
Fishing line or thin wire
Marbles

THE SCIENCE BEHIND THE TRICK

The wire, weighted by the marbles, puts pressure on the ice. This pressure creates heat that melts a thin strip of ice, letting the wire gradually sink through. But as the wire sinks, the water over it freezes again because heat flows from the warmer water to the cooler ice around it.

Force of wire pressing on thin strip of ice

Ice block

Force of gravity pulls weighted pails down

1 Fill one half of a plastic sandwich box with water and put it into the freezer. Do this the day before you perform your act.

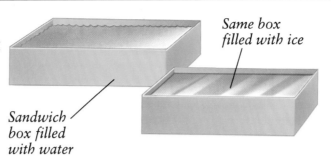

Same box filled with ice

Sandwich box filled with water

3 Make two pails by cutting the bottoms off plastic bottles. Attach each one to the end of a piece of thin wire by poking holes through the plastic.

2 Find two glass jars that still have their lids. Decorate them with magic symbols cut from colored paper.

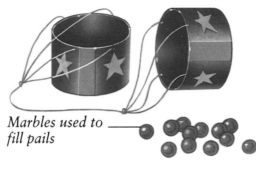

Marbles used to fill pails

WARNING: DO NOT ATTEMPT THIS TRICK ON A HOT DAY!

WHAT YOU NEED
Cardboard box
Cardboard ★ Glue
Cellophane tape
Colored paper ★ Scissors
Small plastic bags
Straws ★ Large cloth
Marble

INTRODUCING MAGIC MIKE
AND THE
MAGIC MARBLE

The magic marble is under Magic Mike's control. It topples from the box at his command!

Before you do this trick, put the bags on your table and put a cloth over the top to hide them. Put the box on top of one of the bags and balance the marble on top of it. Announce that you will make the marble fall by mind power. Pretend to concentrate hard on the marble and secretly press the other bag. The box will wobble, making the marble fall.

THE SCIENCE
BEHIND THE TRICK

Pushing down on one plastic bag pushes air into the other bag. The pressure of the air makes the bag into a stiff structure, which pushes up the box, making it wobble. The bags are a simple pneumatic (air powered) lifting machine. Air pressure can create all sorts of different structures — anything from a football to a bicycle tire.

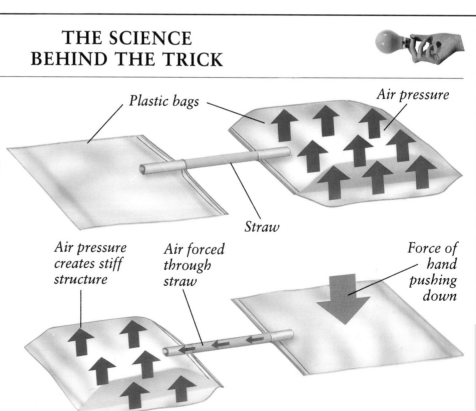

Plastic bags

Air pressure

Straw

Air pressure creates stiff structure

Air forced through straw

Force of hand pushing down

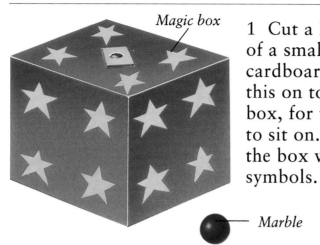

Magic box

Marble

Plastic bag

1 Cut a hole in the middle of a small piece of cardboard. Glue this on top of the box, for the marble to sit on. Decorate the box with magic symbols.

2 Using cellophane tape, seal the openings of two plastic bags so they are airtight. Leave a small hole in the middle for a straw to fit into.

3 Push a straw into the hole of one bag and seal it in with cellophane tape. Blow the bag up and then put the other bag on the other end of the straw.

Tape

Straw

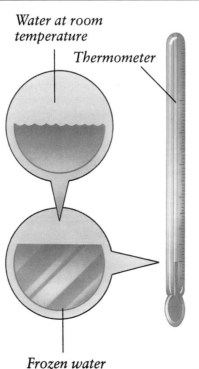

INTRODUCING MAGIC MANDY
AND THE
FROZEN BUILDING

First it's there, then it's gone! Magic Mandy makes a paper building collapse by itself.

Leave the strips of paper in the freezer until the last moment. (Your assistant can bring them to you.) Don't let the audience know they are frozen. Lean the strips against each other on the tray. (Squeeze the tops together to help them stay up.) Cover the "building" with a cardboard box and put it to one side while you do another trick. Remove the box and the building will have collapsed!

WHAT YOU NEED
Cardboard box
Colored paper ★ Glue
Paints or markers
Water ★ Clothespins
Tissue paper ★ Plastic tray

THE SCIENCE BEHIND THE TRICK

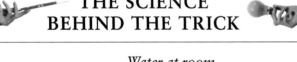

This trick relies on the fact that water, which is a liquid, freezes to make ice, which is a solid. When the water in the strips freezes, the strips turn solid. But as the ice gradually melts, the building collapses.

Water at room temperature

Thermometer

Frozen water

Tray

1 Decorate a tall cardboard box with magic symbols. Cut a hole in the bottom to let it fit over the standing frozen strips.

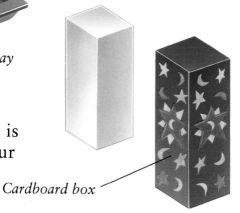

Frozen strips

Cardboard box

2 Find a medium-sized plastic tray. Make sure it is small enough to fit in your freezer.

3 Cut strips of tissue paper. Soak them in water and hang them up to get rid of the excess water. Put them on the tray in the freezer.

INTRODUCING MAGIC MANDY
AND THE
MIND BENDING TRICK

Mind over matter makes the spoon bend in Magic Mandy's hands.

Put a mug filled with boiling water on the tray under the box before you start. After the audience examines the spoon, dip it into the box (and secretly into the hot water) and press it down. Pretend to concentrate on the spoon. Remove the spoon and wave it about to cool it before you let the audience see that it's bent.

WHAT YOU NEED
Cardboard box with lid
Scissors ★ Colored paper
Glue ★ Tray ★ Ceramic
mug ★ Boiling water
(from a kettle) ★ Plastic
spoons

THE SCIENCE BEHIND THE TRICK

Thermosetting plastic, used for most plastic utensils, gets soft when it heats up and sets hard when it cools down. As the plastic warms up, the tiny particles inside are freed from each other and start to move around. When cooled, they move close together again.

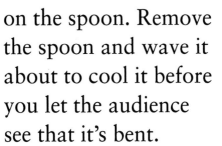

Molecules are closer together at room temperature

Plastic spoon

Heated molecules move apart

1 Cut a hole in the lid of the cardboard box. It must be large enough for a spoon to go through.

Hole lines up with mug of hot water

Spoons

2 Decorate the box with magic symbols. Place it on the tray, lining the hole up with the mug of water.

BE CAREFUL WITH BOILING WATER

3 Just before you do the trick, ask an adult to boil water in a kettle and pour it into the mug.

INTRODUCING MAGIC MANDY
AND THE
VANISHING WAND

It really is a magic wand! Magic Mandy makes it disappear into thin air with a clap of her hands.

Secretly replace your real magic wand with the trick one. Then say that you are going to make your wand disappear so that nobody else can use its powers. Tap it on the table to show that it's solid. Lay it on the table and cover it with a cloth. Pick it up by the ends and then crush it up with a clap of your hands.

WHAT YOU NEED
Small saw ★ Thick wooden dowel or corks Black paper ★ Scissors Glue ★ Cloth ★ Colored pens or crayons

THE SCIENCE BEHIND THE TRICK

Tubes make good supports (for example, tent poles) because they don't bend easily. When you tap the trick wand it feels solid because the paper tube doesn't bend. But if you twist it as you push you remove much of the shape's strength and it crushes easily.

Push down and twist

1 Using a small saw, carefully cut two short pieces of dowel (or cork).

Dowel or cork

Black paper

2 Cut out a piece of black paper. A good size is 12 in. (30 cm) by 8 in. (20 cm).

3 Roll the paper into a stiff tube. Insert the dowel pieces in each end and glue.

Dowel glued to end of wand

4 Decorate the wand using colored pens or crayons.

INTRODUCING MAGIC MIKE
AND THE
MAGIC BANDS

One loop or two? Only Magic Mike knows as his volunteers cut the mysterious bands.

First, pick up the untwisted band and carefully cut it in half lengthways. (It is easier to cut if you pierce a hole in the middle of the band first.) Show the two resulting bands to your audience. Now ask for two volunteers. Ask them each to cut one of the other bands lengthways. One will end up with a single long twisted band and the other with two loops magically linked together!

WHAT YOU NEED
Colored paper
Cellophane tape
Two pairs of scissors

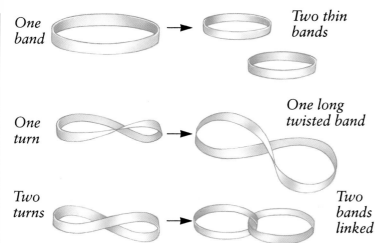

One band → *Two thin bands*

One turn → *One long twisted band*

Two turns → *Two bands linked*

This weird effect happens because each band has a different number of edges and faces. It's really a trick of mathematics. To see the difference between the bands, put your finger on a face of each band and slide it along until you get back to the start.

1 Make a long strip of paper by joining shorter strips. Tape the ends together to make a band.

2 Make another band, but this time turn one end over before taping the ends together.

This is called a Möbius strip.
3 Make a third band, but this time turn one end over twice before taping the ends.

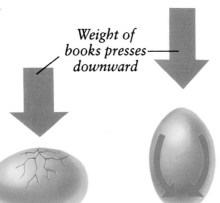

WHAT YOU NEED

Books ★ Sheet of cardboard ★ Scissors Paints ★ Cardboard tubes Modeling clay ★ Eggs

INTRODUCING MAGIC MIKE
AND THE
SUPER STRONG EGG

We all know that eggs are very delicate. But Magic Mike's egg isn't! He tricks it into being as strong as iron.

Start with your base and two supports on your table, with the pile of books next to it. Announce that your magic egg can hold up the pile of heavy books. Take the egg from your pocket and put it on the clay ring. Now add the books one by one. Amazingly, the egg does not break. Break the egg afterwards to show it's real.

THE SCIENCE BEHIND THE TRICK

The egg is very strong because its ends form two tall arch shapes. The arch is very good at holding up weight, which is why this shape is used for bridges. The egg on its side would be much weaker.

Weight of books presses downward

Load is spread across egg

1 Make a pile of large books. You'll need tall, wide ones to fit between the egg and the supports. Five or six books are enough — too many and the egg will break!

Books

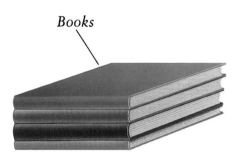

Egg

Modeling clay

Supports

Cardboard

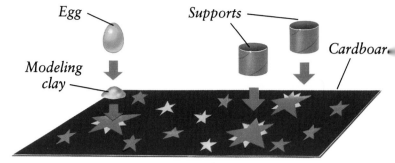

2 Cut a large sheet of cardboard — about 20 in. (50 cm) × 16 in. (40 cm). Decorate it with magic symbols. For the supports cut two cardboard tubes the same height as the egg. Place them at one end of the sheet and a ring of modeling clay at the other (to hold the egg upright).

INTRODUCING MAGIC MIKE
AND THE
DISAPPEARING JAR

Keep your eye on that jar! First it's there, then it's gone. Surely it hasn't gone through the table?

Pick up the sheet of paper and put it over the jar. Now carefully scrunch it around the jar, twisting as you do it, so that it takes on the shape of the jar. Pick up the paper and jar, and let the jar slide out and drop into the box at your feet. Put the paper down again and squash it down as though you were forcing the jar through the table.

WHAT YOU NEED
Sheet of paper
Cardboard box
Colored pens or paints
Newspaper ★ Glass jar
with lid

THE SCIENCE
BEHIND THE TRICK

Paper is one of the few materials that can be bent and folded easily. It also stays in shape when it's bent. The scrunched paper keeps its shape, but can be crushed easily.

Paper keeps shape of jar

Paper wrapped around glass jar

24

Decorate a large sheet of paper and a cardboard box with magic symbols made from colored cardboard or painted on. Fill the box with scrunched-up newspaper to make a soft landing for the jar. Find a medium-sized jar with a lid.

Newspaper

Box

Paper

Strong glass jar

INTRODUCING MAGIC MANDY
AND THE
LEVITATING BOXES

And finally! Magic Mandy defies the forces of gravity. The boxes seem to float in the air!

Lay the four boxes on the table, and carefully slide each one away from the next to show your audience that they are not joined together. (Make sure the fishing line is hidden.) After lining the boxes up, ask a volunteer to push on the end box and lift it up. Pull the fishing line tight, and Presto! When your volunteer lets go, the boxes will float without any support.

WHAT YOU NEED
Thin cardboard
Pencil ★ Scissors ★ Glue
Fishing line

THE SCIENCE BEHIND THE TRICK

When you pull the fishing line, it pulls the boxes tightly together. The force of friction between the faces of the boxes stops them from moving. Some bridges are built like this, with concrete pieces held together with steel wires.

Hand squeezes upward

String pulls boxes downward

String pulls boxes together

Friction holds the faces together

GETTING PREPARED

1 Copy this shape onto thin cardboard. Each square should be about 4 in. (10 cm) × 4 in. Cut it out and fold it into a cube, gluing the tabs. Make four cubes in all.

Cardboard

2 Pierce two holes in the center of each box and push a piece of fishing line through all of them. Tie a knot in one end.

Knot

String through boxes

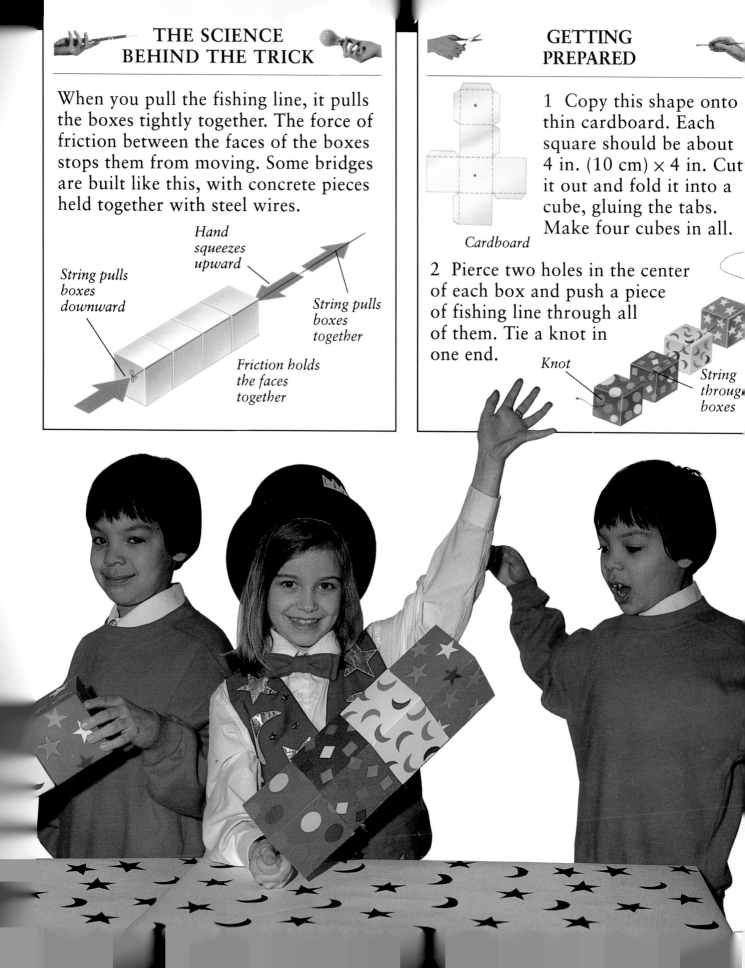

HINTS AND TIPS

Here are some hints and tips for making your props. Good props will make your act look more professional, so spend time making and decorating your props, and look after them carefully. As well as the special props you need for each trick, try to make some general props such as a vest and a magic wand.

Decorate your props with magic shapes cut from colored paper. Paint bottles and tubes with oil-based paint.

You will need cellophane tape and glue to make props. Double-sided tape may also be useful. Thick fabric-based tape is good for joining the edges of boxes together, and it's easy to paint too.

Stenciling is a good way to decorate large areas. Cut magic shapes such as stars and crescent moons out of cardboard. Throw away the shape, but keep the hole! Put the hole over the surface and paint through it with a sponge.

Your act will look more professional if you make a stage setting. This is easy if you have a backdrop to hang behind the stage. A large piece of black cloth is most effective. Use silver paint to stencil on stars and moons. Also decorate pieces of cloth to throw over your table. The overall effect will be dramatic, creating an atmosphere of mystery and magic.

Make your own magician's clothes. Try to find an old hat and vest to decorate. If you can find some silvery material, cut out stars and moons and sew them on. An alternative is to use sequins, or anything else that is shiny and dramatic so you look professional.

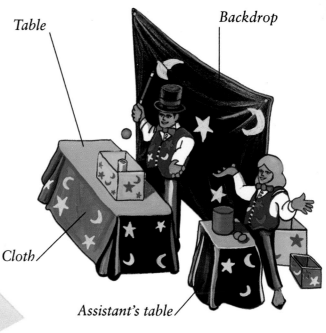

Table

Backdrop

Cloth

Assistant's table

Make a magician's table by draping a cloth over an ordinary table. You can put props out of sight underneath.

GLOSSARY

FREEZING POINT The temperature at which water turns to ice, which is 32°F (0°C) or the temperature below which liquid turns into a solid. Every liquid has its own particular freezing point.

MÖBIUS STRIP A one-sided continuous surface formed by giving a long narrow strip a half twist and then joining the ends. Named after its inventor August Möbius (1790–1868), a German mathematician.

PNEUMATIC MACHINES These are powered by compressed air (air molecules squeezed together into a very small space). The air pushes against a piston that then pushes against a device such as a hammer.

RIGID A structure is rigid when it is completely stiff and cannot be easily bent one way or the other.

THERMOSETTING PLASTIC A plastic that becomes soft when heated and hardens on cooling. While some plastics can be set again in the same shape after being heated, others take on new properties and cannot be remolded.

INDEX